PETERBOROUGH

Volume 3

A Third Portrait in Old Picture Postcards

by

June and Vernon Bull
Stephen Perry and Roy Sturgess

S.B. Publications
1990

First published in 1990 by S. B. Publications

5, Queen Margaret's Road, Loggerheads, Nr. Market Drayton, Shropshire, TF9 4EP.

ISBN 1 870708 57 1

Typeset and printed in Great Britain by Geo. R. Reeve Ltd., Wymondham, Norfolk NR18 0BD.

CONTENTS

CONTENTS CONTINUED

ACKNOWLEDGEMENTS

The authors are indebted to the following people without whose help this book would not have been possible.

Mildred Julyan;
The late Messrs. Harry Miles and John Jack Gaunt;
Brian White for help with the text;
Beverley Spridgeon for typing the script;
John Setchfield for the loan of the postcard on page 24;
Gillian Jackson for editing the text;
Steve Benz for additional editing and marketing.

BIBLIOGRAPHY

"Peterborough" by H.F. Tebbs: The Oleander Press;
"How the City has Changed" by H.F. Tebbs: Peterborough Standard;
"The Peterborough Directory": Geo. C. Caster, Peterborough 1892;
"Fifty Years of Progress" by W.T. Mellows: Peterborough Municipal Jubilee, Peterborough Standard;
"Century Story 1854–1954": Peterborough Advertiser;
"Peterborough Story Through 125 Years of News with the Peterborough Advertiser"; 1980;
"Peterborough Trams" by G.D. Austin: Great Peterborough Arts Council 1978;
"Railways of Peterborough" by Richard Dane: Greater Peterborough Arts Council 1978;
"Rail Centres – Peterborough" by Peter Waszak: Ian Allan Ltd.;
"Aviation in Northamptonshire" by Michael L. Gibson: Northamptonshire Libraries;
"Werrington Through the Ages" by Judy Bunten and Alfred Savage;
"The Imperial Gazetteer of England and Wales" by John Marius Wilson, 6 Volumes: A. Fullerton & Co. 1870;
"Peterborough Advertiser" – weekly periodical held on 35mm film at Peterborough Central Library.

INTRODUCTION

Following the publication of Peterborough: A Portrait in Old Picture Postcards, in July, 1988, and Volume Two, in May, 1989, the interest generated by these books inevitably lead to the question – was there scope for a third volume? The authors met one evening to see if they had enough interesting material for Volume Three – the wealth of marvellous images that are shown on these pages are proof of their success. Postcards of streets and buildings are easy to find compared to those with a social history content. This volume concentrates on people and events rather than topography. All the postcards are rare, some are very rare. Each collector wrote up his own postcards, giving the editors the task of making the final selection.

The book has been designed in two parts: firstly, to feature street scenes, businesses and village life and the second part features various aspects of social history from the first three decades of this century. Where appropriate, the book has been cross-referenced with Volumes One and Two. Every card has some social significance, and the authors – although local historians – demonstrate different approaches when doing research. For instance, Roy Sturgess, not being a Peterborian, tends to set his cards in a wider social history. This is what makes collecting so personal and fascinating.

We hope you enjoy the result and note our joint request – never throw away any paper ephemera. If it is paper and of local interest, please let one of us see it, before consigning it to the dustbin. Please forgive us our mistakes! There are many sources and any one may mislead; memory can be deceptive and even eyesight may be fugitive. If you can supply further information about any aspect of any of these postcards, do let us know, we should be delighted to hear from you.

June and Vernon Bull,
Stephen Perry,
Roy Sturgess.

September 1990

AERIAL VIEW FROM THE WEST, c. 1936

To obtain the best from an aerial view, one must compare it with a large-scale map. The value of these postcards is now appreciated. There were at least three good sets for Peterborough, issued in the 1930s. This one shows the central part of the city, that has become Queensgate: locate St. John's Church in line with the Cathedral – the new development now fills the centre of the long block behind it. All the post-war changes may be traced – with patience!

(R.J. Sturgess collection).

THE PETERBOROUGH EXPRESS

THE PETERBOROUGH EXPRESS, c. 1905

An example of a novelty postcard, this design carried a suitable mailed greeting with a flap on the engine which could be lifted to reveal a concertina of some splendid views of Edwardian Peterborough. It would have cost a ½d to post, or 1d if a message was written on the reverse.

(J. and V. Bull collection)

I have just arrived at PETERBORO'

"I HAVE JUST ARRIVED AT PETERBOROUGH", c. 1905

By rail, of course! Adding a local overprint was one method that the firm of Valentines of Dundee could use to make a design go further. This example is better drawn than most of them. The aristocratic "masher", sucking his cane handle, stands less chance of capturing the lady's attention than the copper! The flash of underskirt was probably considered to be a bit saucy in those days. The message on the back of the card is a happy one . . . . "Connie come out with me every day".

(R.J. Sturgess collection)

CHARLES DICKENS: A PETERBOROUGH VISITOR, c. 1902

Dickens performed one of his famous readings in Peterborough, which confirms his connection with the city. This beautiful, chromolithographed postcard, printed in Saxony, was sent to thank a lady in Liskeard, Cornwall for a donation to the "Fresh Air Fund". It is ironic that a charity should use a postcard depicting someone as uncharitable as Dickens. He was not polite about the city, nor about the lady who served him with "a petrified bun of enormous antiquity" at the station . . . . he then cried in his tea. He has been reported as saying that "Peterborough is the back door to nowhere".

(R.J. Sturgess collection)

4

PETERBOROUGH NORTH (G.N.R.) STATION, c. 1905

The picture shows a Great Northern Railway locomotive, Atlantic Class No. 1408, waiting to depart from Peterborough North with a train for King's Cross. There was a service of eight trains a day, running in both directions between Peterborough and King's Cross; an express could make the journey in 1 hour, 45 minutes, whilst stopping trains would take 3 hours, 20 minutes. Platform 6, on the left, was constructed in 1866, when the Midland and Great Northern Railways agreed to share the cost. It opened to passengers on 1st August and, as a result, the Crescent station closed. The canopy must have been well-constructed as it survived an alleged German air attack in August, 1942. On German radio, Lord Haw Haw stated that the Luftwaffe had bombed Peterborough station when, in fact, it was Ramsey that was hit! (See also Volume 1, pages 16–17).

(J. and V. Bull collection).

PETERBOROUGH NORTH STATION AND YARDS, c. 1922

This photograph was taken from Crescent Bridge, looking across towards Peterborough North Station. In the foreground, Ellis & Everard's employees, together with their horse-drawn coal carts, pose for the camera. At the time of Queen Victoria's Jubilee, some 1200 poor people were entertained at a luncheon in the Midland Railway wagon sheds, just to the left. The menu included cold meats, hot potatoes, plum pudding and a pint of beer for each person. The Great Northern hotel can be seen on the right. (See also Volume 2, page 29).

(J. and V. Bull collection).

OPENING OF NEW BRIDGE PETERBORO APRIL 10TH 13 108.

OPENING OF THE CRESCENT BRIDGE, 13th April, 1913

The photograph shows the Mayoress being escorted into the Great Northern Hotel, by the Town Clerk – just visible in the doorway – and the Corporation, together with officials of the Great Northern Railway and other dignitaries. The importance of the occasion is illustrated by the presence of three Police Constables and their Sergeant, which must have been a sizeable proportion of the local force. The event attracted at least two photographers, one of whom may be seen in the left-hand foreground with his rather substantial, portable camera. (See also Volume 2, page 24).

(S. Perry collection)

CARS FOR HIRE

THE "PREMIER" GARAGE,
G.N. STATION APPROACH, PETERBOROUGH.

PREMIER GARAGE, ST. LEONARD'S STREET, c. 1913

The garage was situated in St. Leonard's Street opposite the Station approach. These magnificently-liveried chauffeurs and their charges would have been available for travellers alighting from the Great Northern Railway trains. The garage was managed by Mr. Walter A. Mathew and offered cars for hire, catering especially for weddings. In more recent times, the garage will be remembered as being under the ownership of the Bowering family, and as being situated between the George Hotel and the Registrar's Office. The building was finally demolished in the early 1980s.

(S. Perry collection).

MIDLAND ROAD NURSERY, c. 1918

J.W. Cole & Son, nurserymen and chrysanthemum specialists, delivered plants all over the country. J.W. Cole, a fellow of the Royal Horticultural Society, and his son, M.J. Cole, owned an extensive number of greenhouses and were renowned for their quality chrysanthemums – a fine display is pictured here. Their nursery site is now mainly occupied by Peterborough District Hospital Nurses Homes, in Holdich Street.

(J. and V. Bull collection).

JULYAN'S BICYCLE SHOP, COWGATE, June 1929

The firm originated at 57, Narrow Bridge Street, in 1869, and moved to this shop at 48, Cowgate, in about 1908. The premises in Narrow Bridge Street was also an established outfitters and boot shop, selling hats and caps, ties and collars, woollens and bespoke suits. At Julyan's in Cowgate, one could buy many makes of cycle including Singer, Rayleigh, Rover, James, Triumph, Roulette, Royal Progress, New Ormonde, Alldays and Coventry Cross. It was said that they sold at prices which allowed a mere commission on the nett cost price. George Langham Julyan and his son, Frank Julyan, ran the Cowgate shop. This view shows the welcome given to H.R.H. Prince George, on his visit to the city on 28th June, 1929. The Prince, who later became the Duke of Kent, was on an official visit to lay the foundation stone of the Municipal Buildings in Bridge Street.

(J. and V. Bull collection).

PRIESTGATE, c. 1908

In 1856, Earl Fitzwilliam offered the present Museum building, together with a large plot of land, in exchange for the old Infirmary building in Milton Street. The new Infirmary in Priestgate, where the Museum stands, was used as a fever hospital until 1931, when the Natural History Society took it over. Apparently, Mr. Bodger, a founder member, confessed that the beginnings of the Museum were in boxes under his bed! (See also Volume 1, page 19).

(J. and V. Bull collection).

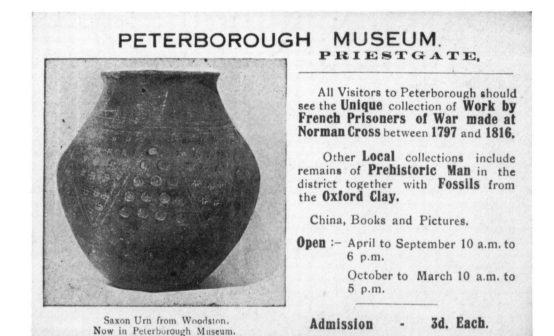

PETERBOROUGH MUSEUM.
PRIESTGATE.

All Visitors to Peterborough should see the **Unique** collection of **Work by French Prisoners of War made at Norman Cross** between 1797 and 1816.

Other **Local** collections include remains of **Prehistoric Man** in the district together with **Fossils** from the **Oxford Clay.**

China, Books and Pictures.

Open :– April to September 10 a.m. to 6 p.m.

October to March 10 a.m. to 5 p.m.

Admission - 3d. Each.

Saxon Urn from Woodston.
Now in Peterborough Museum.

PETERBOROUGH MUSEUM, c. 1920

A very early postcard from the Museum shows the extensive opening hours and the admission fee. Their proudest exhibits remain the same today. The information on the card refers to Oxford Clay, which was the Oxford shale that made Fletton bricks possible. The pot is an indication of the historical importance of the districts of Woodston and Castor, for ceramic skills. In Roman times the area was one of the three most important potteries in Great Britain. Flag Fen now offers Peterborians the chance to look forward to the future – whilst exploring its Bronze Age past.

(R.J. Sturgess collection).

BROAD BRIDGE STREET, c. 1912

At the turn of the century, visitors travelling to Peterborough from the south, once over the Town Bridge, saw this array of shops. On the right-hand side from the right are: at nos. 19 & 20, Arthur Page, house furnishers; nos. 17 & 18, S. & A. Castor, curriers; no. 16, Robert Steward & Sons, plumbers; no. 15, Robertson & Co., Cycle Depot and Riding School; no. 14, J. Emerton, tailor and cab proprietor; at no. 13, Charles Hayward, clerk, and Jonathan Bains, a tailor; no. 12 was the Saracen's Head public house, run by Isaac Dell and, finally, the City Temperance Hotel, run by Mrs. Meehan, in the centre of the picture. On the opposite side, from the left is Owen William Cutlack, Bridge House, Broad Street, J.A. Herbert, clothier and trade valuer, the Boat Inn, run by James Hutchinson, and the Rose & Crown, run by John Marshall.

(J. and V. Bull collection).

S. & A. CASTOR, 17–18 BROAD BRIDGE STREET, c. 1915

S. & A. Castor, established in 1884, were curriers, leather merchants, boot manufacturers and wholesalers. They also had premises in Midgate. The firm was renowned for the quality of its goods and the large selection of styles that were offered. These included the "Lilian", "Institute", "Huggey" and "Esperansh", which were just some of their best-sellers. Samuel and Arthur Castor lived in Wentworth Villas, in London Road.

(J. and V. Bull collection).

WILLIAMSON'S EXPRESS REMOVALS PANTECHNICON, c. 1930s

Williamson's Furnishing Company used this Leyland pantechnicon for their removals business. The vehicle has solid tyres and an open cab. Note the telephone number on the side of the cab – 182; the office was in Market Place. (See Volume 2, page 20). According to the details given on the side of the van, long-distance removals were achieved at the rate of 100 miles a day. The trailer appears to be a flat truck carrying a "demountable" container which could be transferred on to a railway wagon for longer journeys. The container would then be collected at the most convenient station for onward transport to its destination.

(R.J. Sturgess collection).

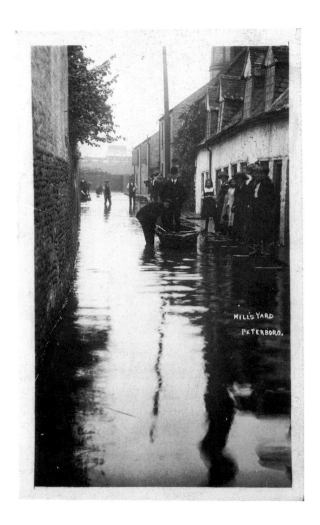

HILL'S YARD, PETERBORO.

HILL'S YARD, August 1912

Hill's yard was within a stone's throw of the River Nene, off Bridge Street. In August 1912, severe flooding was experienced by the inhabitants of this and many of the other yards which ran parallel to it. On this occasion, the occupants of the houses had moved most of their possessions to the upstairs rooms, where they lived until the floodwaters receded. One resident reported that water had reached the top of her table legs and described her existence by saying "we are having a lively time upstairs"! (See also pages 66 and 67; Volume 1, pages 50 and 53; and Volume 2, page 100).

(S. Perry collection).

THE GRAND HOTEL, c. 1901

The Grand Hotel was situated in Wentworth Street. It comprised of separate assembly rooms, which were thoroughly fitted with every convenience for balls, concerts and public meetings. The Hotel also boasted the handsomest smoking room in the Midlands! Suites and apartments were furnished by Maple & Co. In 1901, the proprietor was Mrs. M. Hopwood.

(J. and V. Bull collection).

THE METHODIST CHURCH, WENTWORTH STREET, c. 1905

The Church stood on a site which had been partly occupied by an earlier chapel, built in 1834. This handsome Church was founded in 1874, with seats for more than a thousand people, and was built at a cost of £5,000. In July, 1874, two memorial stones were laid – one by John Howitt, Mayor of Nottingham, and the other by Mr. John Poles of Alwalton. During the foundation ceremony, papers and journals were placed in a bottle and laid in a cavity. The bottle contained: two Peterborough newspapers; a paper about Methodists in Peterborough, written by Mr. R. Bright, a chemist of Bridge Street; plus three Wesleyan journals. The Church was demolished in the 1970s, to make way for offices.

(J. and V. Bull collection).

ST. PETER'S COLLEGE, c. 1912

An example of postcards on postcards! This card shows how do-it-yourself greetings cards could be made. Two photographs of the exterior and two of the interior are arranged with some holly leaves and a seasonal greeting to make an unusual Christmas card for the use of staff and students of this teacher training college. It is situated in City Road but is now used as offices, known as Peterscourt. (See also Volume 1, page 35, and Volume 2, page 76).

(R.J. Sturgess collection).

Old Scarlett, died 1594, in his 98th year.　　Peterborough Cathedral.

YOV SEE OLD SCARLETT'S PICTVRE STAND ON HIE
BVT AT YOVR FEETE HERE DOTH HIS BODY LIE
HIS GRAVESTONE DOTH HIS AGE AND DEATH TIME SHOW
HIS OFFICE BY THES TOKENS YOV MAY KNOW
SECOND TO NONE FOR STRENGTH AND STVRDYE LIMM
A SCAREBABE MIGHTY VOICE WITH VISAGE GRIM
HEE HAD INTRED TWO QVEENES WITHIN THIS PLACE
AND THIS TOWNES HOVSE HOLDERS IN HIS LIVES SPACE
TWICE OVER; BVT AT LENGTH HIS OWN TVRN CAME
WHAT HEE FOR OTHERS DID FOR HIM THE SAME
WAS DONE; NO DOVBT HIS SOVLE DOTH LIVE FOR AYE
IN HEAVEN; THO HERE HIS BODY CLAD IN CLAY.

Pentney

"OLD SCARLETT"

Robert Scarlett, known as "Old Scarlett", is pictured above the West Door of Peterborough Cathedral. He is best known for burying two Queens, namely, Katherine of Aragon and Mary, Queen of Scots. Their bodies were later removed and interred at Westminster Abbey. Old Scarlett died on 2nd July, 1594, aged 98, and is himself buried at the Cathedral. In 1891, when the marble pavement was to be laid in the choir, the vault of Katherine of Aragon was uncovered and her coffin seen. In 1895, the present slab of Irish marble was given by all the "Katherines" of the city who chose to share the cost. The stone, weighing about a ton, is inscribed with Queen Katherine's coat of arms, her name and cross.

(J. and V. Bull collection).

MARKET SQUARE, 22nd June, 1911

The celebrations were for the Coronation of Their Majesties King George V and Queen Mary. George V succeeded to the throne on the death of his father, Edward VII, on 8th May, 1910. Almost in the centre of this view, Bishop Frank Theodore Woods may be seen and, four places to his left, stands the Mayor, Councillor O.E. Crawley, and then the Town Clerk, Mr. W. Mellows. In the centre background, the premises under construction was to be for Boots the Chemists; this site is now occupied by Burger King.

(J. and V. Bull collection).

PETERBOROUGH'S FIRST MOTOR-BUSES, c. 1913

Although the trams continued to run in the city until 1930, the first omnibuses were running as early as 1913. The first omnibus was a 24 h.p. Straker Squire charabanc, with a fixed canopy, six side doors, canvas side curtains and seats for 26 passengers. It made its first appearance on a Sunday in 1913, when crowds gathered in the Market Place to inspect this "wonder carriage". It was driven by Mr. E. Dockrill and its conductor was Mr. J. Allen of Woodston, who later became an Eastern Counties driver. These vehicles were so popular that, within that first year, the Peterborough Traction Co. had a fleet of two charabancs and three saloons, working three services covering 48 miles. In 1931, the Traction Co. merged with the Eastern Counties Omnibus Company.

(J. and V. Bull collection).

LONG CAUSEWAY, 1904

One of Peterborough's busier market days is pictured here; it would have been either a Wednesday or Saturday during the autumn of 1904. Looking down towards Broadway, numerous horse-drawn carts can be seen, making their way to the Market Square to sell agricultural produce such as peas, hay, corn and mangels. The two trams are making their way to the Long Causeway terminus, having travelled from Dogsthorpe and Walton. The building on the left was occupied by R.J. Glass, drapers and milliners. The photograph was taken from a vantage point close to the Sir Henry Pearson Gates monument, which stood in the centre of the Market Square.

(J. and V. Bull collection).

PEPPER'S SHOP, CUMBERGATE, c. 1913

On the left is the window of Pepper's shop, which stood in Cumbergate, opposite the General Post Office. The fine regimented stock of boot and shoes – with sizes and half-sizes displayed on each item – can be clearly seen. This appears to be a rather early building compared with the modern facade of Fairweather's Coal and Coke Office, next door.
(J.T. Setchfield collection).

"POSTCARD" SMITH, WESTGATE, c. 1906

This is the best postcard of a postcard shop yet recorded. Harrison Smith produced and sold postcards from this shop opposite Westgate Church: now, the bus station. His connection with the trade only ended in 1989, when two relatives gave up their Stamford business. Few collectors would not be excited by the mass of postcards on view, and some are able to identify every card, listing the relevant publishers. For example, in the left-hand window, the card that looks like a door-way – near the beer bottle – is the subway that went under Crescent Bridge – this postcard was used as an illustration on page 30 of Volume 2.

(R.J. Sturgess collection).

CLOUDBURST AT PETERBOROUGH 12.6.24. FLOOD SCENE

MIDGATE, 1924

A cloudburst on 12th June, 1924, proved to be a record flood. All the city's streets were badly flooded. The picture shows a Fire Brigade motor-pump dispersing the floodwater. On the left, from left to right, the premises shown were occupied by: C.A. Tebbs, butcher; W.G. Stenson, fishmonger; H.E. Noble, chemist and R.W. North, pork butcher. In the left background is the City of Peterborough Finance Department, where the city accountants, overseers and water rates accounts offices were located. On the right, from right to left, is: T.L. Barrett Ltd., a china and drapery store; F.W. Miller, outfitters; W.F.D. Lewis, cycle factory; the Smiths Arms public house; C. Euchner, pork butchers and the Wheel Inn public house, just before Wheel Yard. Almost all these buildings have gone; Hereward Arcade and Midgate House stand where these shops used to be.

(J. and V. Bull collection).

GAUMONT BRITISH CINEMA STAFF, c. 1938

There is a distinct military-style order of command in this group of doormen and usherettes at the cinema in Broadway. World War 1 medal ribbons are worn by the three men and the one in the middle has a foreman's badge, whilst the other two are numbers two and three. The pill-box-hatted ladies are also numbered – from four to nine. All were eager to serve the public, most of whom went to the pictures at least once a week.

(R.J. Sturgess collection).

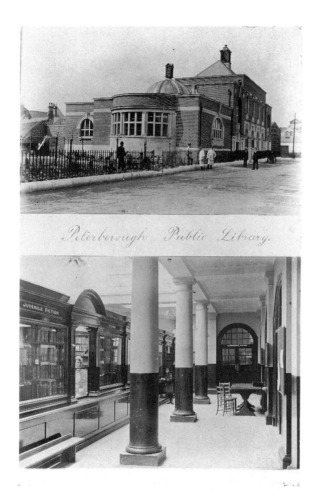

Peterborough Public Library.

PETERBOROUGH PUBLIC LIBRARY, c. 1906

This is one of a series of postcards, published in 1906, when the Public Library, located in Broadway, was opened by its benefactor, Mr. Andrew Carnegie. The fine view of the magnificent interior shows glass-fronted shelves, well-stocked with titles in the juvenile fiction section. The reference room can be seen directly ahead and it is easy to imagine the deafening silence that must have prevailed. The exterior of the building has hardly changed at all from the well-known structure that served the local population until its closure in 1990. (See also Volume 2, page 65).

(S. Perry collection).

W. H. Speechley & Sons, Taxi Proprietors & Contractors,
48 Monument Street, Peterborough.

Petrol & Oils.   Phone 210.   Day & Night Service.

W.H. SPEECHLEY & SONS, c. 1925

W.H. Speechley & Sons were taxi proprietors and contractors. They started their business, in 1912, with horse-drawn carriages and changed to motor-cars after World War 1, in 1919. In this postcard, the proprietor, William Herbert Speechley, is standing on the right, with three drivers who were, from the front to back: Percy Speechley, Bert Speechley and Roy Howe. When William died in the early 1950s, his wife, Fanny, took over the business. They offered a day and night service – any distance – and, as can be seen here, weddings were a speciality.

(J. and V. Bull collection).

SOUVENIR OF ST. MARY'S PARISH, 1911

St. Mary's Church was built in 1861, and cost £2,038. In 1877, St. Mary's was the poorest living, the vicar received just £150 a year, compared with the vicar of St. John's who received £565. The Church had Fitzwilliam as its patron, which was unusual. This postcard was issued to celebrate the Golden Jubilee of the parish. None of the buildings shown here remain today. The New Road site is filled with a steel framework, St. Michael's ended its life as a scout hut but was recently removed to make way for a new road system, whilst St. James' has also gone and Eastgate has modern houses and some pre-war council properties. (See also Volume 1, page 46).

(R.J. Sturgess collection).

BARRASS MEMORIAL HALL, c. 1907

The photograph was taken just after construction of the Chapel and Barrass Memorial Hall had been completed. The Fellowship moved to this site in Park Road after the Chapel and hall in Queen Street had been destroyed by fire, in 1905. (See Volume 2, pages 95 and 96). The hall, which had seen much use over the years, was demolished in 1988, to make way for a modern office block. At the same time, the Chapel was completely altered to accommodate the hall and sanctuary. (See also Volume 1, page 86).

(S. Perry collection).

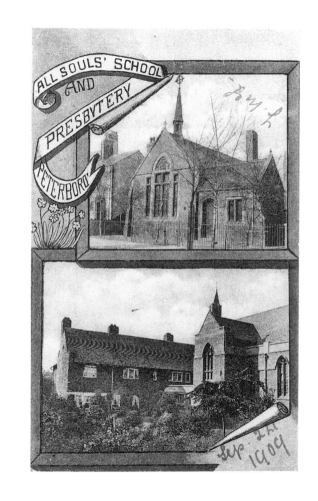

ALL SOULS SCHOOL
AND PRESBYTERY, c. 1909

The top view shows the Roman Catholic All Souls School, built in 1893 in Manor House Street. It cost £1,000 in its entirety, and was built by a Mr. Hammond. When opened there were about 50 pupils although it was reputed to be able to accommodate 150. The bottom view shows the Presbytery, which opened in 1896. It stands at the west end of All Souls Church, which is located in Park Road; access to the Presbytery may be gained from Geneva Street. The Church, School and Presbytery formed the nucleus of the Roman Catholic Community, at this time.

(S. Perry collection).

CROMWELL ROAD, c. 1915

This is a splendid view of the Steam Engine Inn, located on the corner of Russell Street and Cromwell Road. During World War 1, troops billeted in nearby Gladstone Street, Russell Street, Bright Street and Lincoln Road used to have their after-dinner pint in this Allsopp's and Burton public house. Note the advertisements for Allsopp's pale ale and Greers whisky. Today, the Inn is known as The Basant.

(J. and V. Bull collection).

PHONE 306

A.F.TEE. HAULAGE CONTRACTOR. PETERBOROUGH

A.F. TEE, HAULAGE CONTRACTOR, c. 1927

Alfred Frederick Tee, of 67, Taverners Road, was better known as "T" for Transport Furniture Removals. He started a local collection and delivery service for commercial and private goods, using these two lorries. The business became established in the mid-1920s and survives to this day.

(J. and V. Bull collection).

11, LIME TREE AVENUE, 1915

Dolly Judd stands outside her home, in April 1915. Notice the sign for fresh eggs, which could be purchased for a shilling a dozen. (See also Volume 1, page 95).

(J. & V. Bull collection).

Garden at Rosebank, Kindergarten.

HIGH SCHOOL FOR GIRLS
PETERBOROUGH

HIGH SCHOOL FOR GIRLS, c. 1908

The school and kindergarten stood on an L-shaped site fronting Park Road. Both buildings came down to make way for blocks of flats that now fill most of the block. Radcliffe House, built on the old orchard, is still a private residence and took up the north corner. A commotion arose when these two Victorian houses were demolished. Only one house of that type now stands in this part of Park Road.

(S. Perry collection).

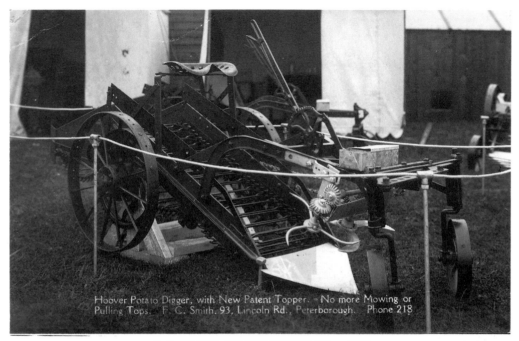

Hoover Potato Digger, with New Patent Topper. No more Mowing or Pulling Tops. F. C. Smith, 93, Lincoln Rd., Peterborough. Phone 218.

F.C. SMITH, 93 LINCOLN ROAD, c. 1928

The caption on the postcard explains that this piece of machinery is a "Hoover Potato Digger, with New Patent Topper. No more Mowing or Pulling Tops". Presumably, the machine was available from F.C. Smith. Mechanisation of agricultural work was hastened after 1876, when the employment of children below eight years of age was made illegal. After the collapse of the grain trade in the 1880s, Peterborough survived by turning to specialised crops such as potatoes. The intense labour needed at harvesting time would have been reduced with the introduction of this machine. No. 93, Lincoln Road is now a private house.

(R.J. Sturgess collection).

MOTOR-CYCLE FL 1693, c. 1919

Readers with an interest in mechanical devices will appreciate this vehicle – a more sturdy machine one will not see. The reverse of the postcard notes that W. Edwin Cole, of Taverners Road, was its creator. A check of local photographers' records revealed that S.E. Cole of Taverners Road was one of the people who went up in the plane that crashed at Werrington. (See page 52).

(R.J. Sturgess colection).

COUNTY SCHOOL, PETERBORO.

THE COUNTY SCHOOL FOR GIRLS, c. 1916

The school was built on a 1½ acre site, at Lincoln Road and Cobden Avenue, now Lincoln Gate. The opening ceremony, in 1911, was performed by the Marchioness of Exeter. At the time, Lt. Col. C.I. Strong was the first Chairman of the County Education Committee, Miss K. Wragge was headmistress and Miss H.S. Hough was second mistress. It began with 200 secondary pupils; in 1920, this had increased to 436. The Junior School had premises opposite, which had six large classrooms and a cloakroom. During World War 1, the School raised money for the upkeep of two Belgian refugee families in the city. In 1922, the tuition fees were: 2 guineas per term for girls from the County; 3 guineas for those from outside. Boarding fees were £30 to 36 guineas per annum; the Boarding School was located at "The Lawns", Thorpe Road, where the Registry Office is now.

(J. and V. Bull collection).

THE MILL, PETERBORO.

THE MILL, MILLFIELD, c. 1915

A close-up view of Adam's Mill shows the detail on this six-sailed tower mill, with its six-bladed fantail and stage. Notice the domed cap with its pointed finial and knob on top – this is known as an ogee cap. The faint letters painted on the roof read: "Corn merchant . . . . Straw offals" (dregs). The card was posted in 1915, the same year that the mill was converted to electricity and lost its unique set of six sails. Twenty years ago, the remains stood in Adam's garage yard, but, like the cottages, have now vanished. (See also Volume 1, page 99).

(R.J. Sturgess collection).

LINCOLN ROAD, c. 1914

Photographed at the junction with Burghley Road – then Lincoln Road East – this view shows an interesting variety of Edwardian costumes. The photographer must have had clothes in mind when he took this picture, as the hand-cart from Sketchley's Cleaning and Dye Works is on one of its rounds. Notice the unusually positioned post-box sited in the middle of the road!

(J. and V. Bull collection).

DOGSTHORPE ROAD CO-OP, c. 1907

The growing importance of Peterborough attracted the Co-operative Society in 1876. The Dogsthorpe branch served a relatively quiet part of the city, and stood on the corner of Princes Street. Postmarked March, 1907, this card must have been sent very soon after it opened. (See also Volume 2, page 44).

(R.J. Sturgess collection).

PETERBOROUGH ·
THE LOW FARM FROM THE EAST·

THE LOW FARM, FENGATE, c. 1891

A view that predates the advent of picture postcards in 1894, was used for this postcard issued at the beginning of this century. The Low Farm was demolished and, in 1901, an Isolation Hospital was built on this site. At the time, scarlet fever, diphtheria and other infectious diseases were rife. The hospital offered thirty beds, was self-contained and had three separate divisions open to patients from the city and surrounding districts. Dr. Robert Jolly (1854–1916) was actively concerned with the building of the Isolation Hospital or sanitorium, which is now St. Peter's Hospital.

(J. and V. Bull collection).

43

OLD MILL AND MILL HOUSE, FENGATE, c. 1903

The old post-mill was situated on the banks of Car Dike, once a Roman canal, which ran from the River Nene up through Park Meadow Farm and on into the Fens. Robert Bodger was the miller and baker there until 1884, when it was sold to a local farmer named Frederick W. Holdich, whose grandfather had previously owned the mill between 1809 and 1852. In 1919, the mill was destroyed by fire and the site is now beneath the Frank Perkins Parkway and Fengate Industrial Estate.

(J. and V. Bull collection).

aug. 9. 1915.

EASTFIELD ROAD, c. 1915

The Peterborough Steam Laundry Co. Ltd.'s delivery van is seen here at the junction of Princes Gardens. The Laundry was located to the west of Cowies, the Volvo garage in Crawthorne Road. After World War 2, it became Crawthorne Laundries (P'boro) Ltd., and had moved to premises in Park Road – where Elizabeth Court now stands. At one time, the proprietor was Herbert Butcher, M.P. for Holland and Boston. The Steam Laundry offered many features including: highest class work, moderate charges, soft water only used, perfect sanitation. Also open-air drying wherever possible. In addition, all washing materials of the best quality with no chemicals used. Customers' property was insured against fire. Clean and soiled linen never came into contact. Linen was sent home thoroughly aired. Plus regular collection and delivery by the Company's vans.

(J. and V. Bull collection).

PASTON, NR PETERBORO.

PASTON, c. 1908

This view shows Paston Ridings and a large farmhouse, which was once the home of the Crowson and Darby families. The road used to lead on to join up with Newborough Road. The large wall in the centre hides Paston rectory. Three bungalows – nos. 30, 32 and 34 Paston Ridings – now occupy the site of the farmhouse. Under Peterborough Extension Order (1928), which came into force on 1st April, 1929, Paston Ward was created and this added three members to the council.

(J. and V. Bull collection).

46

WALTON, c. 1908

To the north, beyond Rhubarb Bridge, Lincoln Road becomes Lincoln Road, Walton, and house numbers begin at No. 1 again. The wall on the left is at No. 247, "St. Bedes", the fourth house from the juction of Sages Lane. It was the home of Albert John Carnt, Director of Peter Brotherhood Ltd., and Alan Hubert Carnt, an engineer; a former resident was Rev. R.K. Gaskell. In 1901, Walton's population was 556; the house on the right was occupied by George Batty, a farm foreman; the next by Stephen Cartland, a chauffeur, and the next by Miss Sarah Ann Harrison, who took delivery of letters and parcels. Collection times were 8 a.m., 2.30 p.m. and 5 p.m. Beyond Miss Harrison's home was the old Royal Oak public house. The present Royal Oak was built in 1935–36, on land owned by G.W. Heading, a farmer. The railway station was located round the corner, to the left.

(J. and V. Bull collection).

THE DUCK POND, WALTON, c. 1930

Many residents will have childhood memories of days spent playing around this pond, near Brown's Farm, during an interlude from train-spotting at nearby Walton Crossing. When this picture was taken, the houses on the left, in Marholm Road, had been built only recently – in direct contrast to the old farm buildings and now outdated style of haystack. Notice the old style road sign inviting motorists to halt before crossing onto Lincoln Road.

(S. Perry collection).

AFTER THE GREAT STORM AT WALTON, PETERBORO
MARCH 28TH 1916.

THE GREAT STORM AT WALTON, 28th March, 1916

One of the worst storms this century was recorded on Tuesday, 28th March, 1916. It started in the early morning and the storm-force winds continued unabated until 6 p.m. Heavy snowfall followed, and about 60–70 telegraph poles were reported to be down between Peterborough and Deeping. This picture, taken by T.S. Wilson, shows the aftermath at Walton, with a stranded tram unable to complete its journey!

(J. and V. Bull collection).

After the Great Floods April 1916.

AFTER THE GREAT FLOODS, April, 1916

The exact location is obscure but the flood was the result of the storm of 28th March, 1916. Photographed by Etcher & Hall, local men who ran a press service, the cameraman captured the moment when the abandoned motor-car, FL 1058, is passed by EW 1032, which is still functioning and desperate to keep the engine running to avoid water entering the exhaust pipe. The geography of Peterborough, being surrounded by fifty thousand acres of fen, invited regular flooding. This problem was not solved until the 1950s.

(R.J. Sturgess collection).

MR EWENS BIPLANE AFTER THE ACCIDENT JULY 1st 1912, AT PETERBOROUGH

THE "DAILY MAIL" AIRMAN AT PETERBOROUGH, 1st July, 1912

To encourage British aviation, the Daily Mail had offered prizes for air races and first flights betweeen major towns and cities of Britain. Mr. Ewen was an early aviator who was the first airman to land at Peterborough – on 29th June, 1912. (See Volume 2, page 102). To commemorate the event, he was presented with a rose bowl by the ex-mayor, and a lucky silver horseshoe by little Queenie Topham Haynes. On 1st July, after giving some flying displays, Mr. Ewen left for Lincoln but, just after take-off, the biplane failed to gain height and crashed. The picture shows the wreckage and the Daily Mail van in the background. Fortunately, Mr. Ewen was uninjured and, after essential repairs, was able to take off again on 4th July.

(R.J. Sturgess collection).

This is the one
that fell at
Peterboro

AIR CRASH AT WERRINGTON, 1920

Many local readers of the Advertiser had free rides from Werrington's civil aerodrome, run by Mr. Summerfield. Those taking advantage of the "freebies" included Frank Loomes, the editor, and Basil Riley, who was still dealing with advertising in the paper, in 1954. One summer day in 1920, Avro G-EAR crashed, killing the pilot and his passengers. The trite message written on the front of this postcard refers to the crash. The card was sent in 1921.

(R.J. Sturgess collection).

Werrington, Peterborough.

WERRINGTON, c. 1906

The view shows Werrington Green, photographed from the east, with Hall Lane in the distance. On the right is the Wesleyan Methodist Church. The first white, thatched cottage on the right has since been demolished. To the left of the centre, beyond the large house, stood the cottage of W. Talbot, a collar and harness-maker, who would have had a model horse in his window symbolising the owner's trade.

(J. and V. Bull collection).

FLAX FACTORY, PEAKIRK, c. 1916

This small factory produced linen from flax and was situated in Peakirk. The exact location is unknown, but it is possible that it was sited close to the railway station. The photograph shows a work force of one man and twenty seven women. All are wearing the standard overalls of the period. Notice the kitten and the hank of flax in the foreground.

(R.J. Sturgess collection).

GROWN WITH
HADFIELD'S
CHEMICAL GUANO
BY MR. E.E. BLAND
EYE, PETERBOROUGH

Mr. E. E. Bland, High Street, Eye, Peterborough, writes:—"The above yielded 13 tons per acre and out of over 50 tons ware I only got 2 tons seed and chats. I am now lifting 11 acres and several growers say they never saw a better crop for this season. There was not an ounce of farm-yard manure used."

HADFIELD'S CHEMICAL GUANO, c. 1933

George Hadfield imported guano (bird manure) from the South Pacific or South America. Established in Liverpool, in 1820, they operated a bone, fertilizer and vitriol works. Farmers like Mr. Bland of Eye were photographed with eye-catching giant crops and the resulting pictures were used on advertising postcards. Ironically, this postcard, sent in October, 1933, asked the recipient to send a wagon-load of the other organic staple (stable manure) to Partington! It also has a strange note in red ink ". . . tell Balls to load CLG & put plenty of offal . . ."

(R.J. Sturgess collection).

55

FEN FARMING CO. LTD., c. 1925

This fine agricultural scene shows threshing in the yard, using a machine operated by a steam engine. The men move the crop – but a young woman bags it. Notice the large pile of coal against the barn and the fine detail of the young boy making friends with an enormous sow at the foot of the ladder. The postcard is rare and more interesting because it is initialled, on the back, by the managing director . . . E. A. G. The Company still operates from Thorney.

(R.J. Sturgess collection).

BEEHIVE MAKER, c. 1905

A maker of hives, said to be in the Peterborough district, but also possibly from Whittlesey or even Bourne. There are a dozen types to choose from, in this photograph, including two straw-rope designs developed from the early cone-shaped mediæval hives. Such hives would have filled the bee boles that can still be seen in Thorpe Manor's walls. This postcard is an important social document that could be unique.

(R.J. Sturgess collection).

SMITH BROS.' WAGON, c. 1920

Heavy horses are making a come back in this age of ecological awareness. Their physical beauty, and the associated traditional crafts of the harness-maker and the wheelwright, make this an attractive and collectable postcard. Smith Bros. are still listed in the telephone directory – at Must Farm, King's Dyke, which runs beside the railway line out towards Whittlesey. Notice the pole on the left – and indication that they were connected to the electricity supply, even though they were so isolated.

(R.J. Sturgess collection).

THE BRICKFIELDS, c. 1906

Brickmaking was established at Fletton in 1877; they were made entirely by a hand process from plastic clay. Underneath that plastic clay lay Oxford shale that made semi-dry bricks possible. New Hoffman kilns replaced the old Scottish kilns towards the end of the century. The London Brick Co. entered the scene in 1922 and, by the end of 1928, decimated the industry. Recently, such brickfields have been reduced to a mere "pile of bricks". This is a very rare postcard and a collector's "gem".

(R.J. Sturgess collection).

Council Schools, Old Fletton.

OLD FLETTON COUNCIL SCHOOL, c. 1912

Huntingdonshire County Secondary School, also known as Old Fletton Board School, stood in High Street, Fletton. It was established in 1910 by Hunts. County Council, to provide secondary education for boys and girls from the northern parts of the county. Originally, accommodation was provided for 100 pupils but extensions, in 1915 and 1921, raised this to 180. On the right of this picture is Fletton Fields and the building is Scottings General Stores. The school was demolished in the late 1960s to make way for industrial units.

(J. and V. Bull collection).

LADIES FOOTBALL TEAM, PETERBOROUGH CINEMAS, 9th November, 1934

Ladies football is not a modern phenomenon. On Thursday, 9th November, 1934, a match was played between ladies representing Peterborough Cinemas and Marks and Spencer. The match took place on Fletton United football ground. Admission for adults was 6d. and for children 3d., and profits were in aid of Mayor A.E. Fletcher's Unemployment Fund . . . .

(R.J. Sturgess collection).

NENE VALE LADIES FOOTBALL CLUB, 9th November, 1934

. . . . This was the team that represented Marks and Spencer in the match. The result is not known, but two fine collectable postcards remain as souvenirs of the event.

(R.J. Sturgess collection)

London Express crossing River at Peterboro'. *P.S.*

RAILWAY BRIDGE AND THE RIVER NENE, c. 1905

A Stirling 8ft Single of the Great Northern Railway G3 class (one of the last six Stirling Singles to be built, during 1894–5), crosses the original double-tracked bridge over the River Nene, from Peterborough towards London, on the Great Northern Railway main line. This bridge may still be seen today, standing next to a later structure, built when the track was quadrupled. This photograph was probably taken from the footbridge over the mouth of the G.N.R. Dock, which was situated where the Nene Sidings are at present. The signal gantry, just visible through the centre arch of the bridge, was on the London & North Western line, west of the London Road – where the fairground is today. (See also Volume 2, page 6).

(S. Perry collection).

LONDON ROAD, c. 1923

This photograph was taken from the footbridge over the Great Eastern Railway line, which serviced Rugby, Northampton, Leicester, Ely, Cambridge and Norwich, and shows a general view over the Nene. On the right is the junction with Station Road, which leads to Peterborough East station. Notice the hairdressing salon and the advertisement for St. Julien tobacco. (See also Volume 1, page 54).

(J. and V. Bull collection).

REGATTA DAY

Any postcard numbered "62" indicates a long set of views to frustrate collectors! A photographer would have to work hard to capture a more lively scene than this – even at the new rowing course. This view of the east side of the river, by the Town Bridge, is full of activity and shows a coxed four coming in, watched by a smart crowd of spectators. The Patent Safety Ladder Co. can still be found, tucked away at the bottom of Jubilee Street, off Oundle Road. (See also Volume 2, page 5).

(R.J. Sturgess collection).

PETERBOROUGH FLOODS   AUG 1912, No 3

RIVER NENE FLOODS, August, 1912

A week of flood and ruin – the like of which had never before been witnessed in the city – brought about some strange and desolate scenes in the week beginning 26th August. After thirteen and a half hours of non-stop rain, huge inland lakes appeared, one of which extended into Fair Meadow, Bridge Street and reached Goodyer's Yard, Bodger's Yard, Hill's Yard, Baker Street and Globe Street. The Minster precincts and old East station were also flooded. This view shows the L. & N.W.R. line, surrounded by the River Nene which was at an all-time high of 17ft. 6 ins. This level beat the previous record set in 1848, when a boat sailed down Bridge Street to the Golden Lion. In 1912, the residents were so concerned for their livestock that pigs were carried upstairs to safety! Fields of ripe wheat and barley were completely destroyed.
(See also page 16; Volume 1, pages 50 and 53; and Volume 2, Page 100).

(J. and V. Bull collection).

OUNDLE ROAD, WOODSTON, August, 1912

In this view of the floods, a coal cart is passing under the bridge at the junction of London Road and Oundle Road, looking towards Woodston. The cart belonged to Hunting & Co. Ltd. who were situated at the G.N.R. wharf. The water level under the bridge is several inches deep, as car and cart try to negotiate a way through! The floodwater started to subside on Thursday, 29th August, when the weather was reported to be sunny with a stiff and pleasant breeze.
(See also Volume 1, page 53).

(R.J. Sturgess collection).

OUNDLE ROAD, PETERBOROUGH.   4.

OUNDLE ROAD, c. 1930

The row of shops – which included a tobacconists, a haberdashers and a shoe shop – has now been converted into a small supermarket. The building on the other corner of Jubilee Street was built in 1887. Beyond these houses, one can now see the outlines of the modern sugar factory.

(R.J. Sturgess collection).

UNVEILING WAR MEMORIAL LYCH GATE, WOODSTON. APRIL 3rd, 1920

UNVEILING WOODSTON WAR MEMORIAL, 3rd April, 1920

For several years after World War 1, and in all parts of the country, money was raised so that memorials could be erected in memory of those who had given their lives for their country. Instead of the usual stone memorial, the people of Woodston chose to erect a lychgate. As one in three of those who went to war were killed in World War 1, the unveiling ceremony probably reached the hearts of everyone present. The gate still stands.

(R.J. Sturgess collection)

THE HUNT, MILTON HALL, c. 1907

The message on the back of this postcard identifies the Master: " . . . The photo was taken on a Monday and a very good one of Mr. Fitzwilliam too . . .." The famous pack of hounds were ancestors of the pack that was chief prizewinner at Redcar in September, 1859. This foxhound show was the first to be open to all England, although showing hounds dates back to the 1760s. The kennels still house a pack whose presence may be heard at mealtime! (See also Volume 1, page 4).

(R.J. Sturgess collection).

B·C·HUCKS AT MILTON PARK MAY 29TH 13¹

B.C. HUCKS AT MILTON PAR, 29th May, 1913

Peterborough had seen its first aeroplane in October, 1911, and experienced its first landing in June, 1912. (See page 51). By 1913, they were getting blasé! B.C. Hucks was a pioneer aviator who travelled the country with his monoplane, giving flying displays at County Shows and other such gatherings. This card was sent by "Postcard" Smith to his brother in Stamford. Within two years, aeroplanes were to be used for the first time as weapons of war, in France.

(R.J. Sturgess collection).

CHURCH HILL, CASTOR, c. 1907

A modern copy taken from the original, this view was used by the Chapel Collectors Centre for advertising. The Chapel is on the right; sold recently, it was stripped out and refitted for use as a commercial office. Its severe facade looks the same, as does the street – apart from some gentrification. Notice the wheelbarrow, a dog and the boots on the right. The cameraman persuaded the ten tots and two men to pose for this photograph but, as the message reads – they were seventy years too early for the Centre! Given away free this postcard is already very collectable.

(R.J. Sturgess collection).

MARY, QUEEN OF SCOTS, c. 1908

Mary, Queen of Scots was executed at Fotheringhay and first buried at Peterborough Cathedral on 1st August, 1587. The message on this card serves her well, dated 4th July, 1908, it reads: "It is the Scottish gentleman that makes an offering and pilgrimage to Fotheringhay. You will see the outline of a wreath in the tree. In less than 24 hours over a thousand people took a portion of it as a souvenir. They were red, white and blue immortelles".

(R.J. Sturgess collection).

ASCENSION DAY PROCESSION, BRIDGE STREET, 21st May, 1914

Ascension Day was celebrated by a procession of clergy, choirs and members of the Church of England Missionary Society to evening service in the Cathedral. The service started in St. John's Church in Church Street, and was directed by Reverend A.F. Maskew with Mr. B. Manders as musical director. The sermon was given by Canon P.H. Bowers, Rector of Market Bosworth. During the Cathedral service, the intense heat caused two of the choristers to faint and they had to be relieved of their duties.

(J. and V. Bull collection).

PETERBOROUGH'S CRIMEAN VETERAN, June, 1913

The picture was taken on 29th June and was posted a few days later on 1st July. It shows the Mayor, John Golby Barford, in his garden with an old soldier who had fought at Crimea, sixty years earlier. The message is surprising: " . . . The old man with Uncle Jim is a Crimean veteran, and wore his medals and then his Indian medals. He was badly shot in the throat and has such a hole still". Uncle Jim was the Mayor, but who was the veteran? "Postcard" Smith sold this card from his Westgate shop within three days of the event.

(R.J. Sturgess collection).

MAYOR & OFFICERS PETERBORO TERRITORIALS, 1913.

PETERBOROUGH TERRITORIALS, June, 1913

Mayor Barford again, but this time he is photographed amongst a group of territorials. This postcard picture must have been taken at the same time as the one on the previous page, for the setting is the same – in the garden of Gayhurst, the Barford family home – and the source is the same, "Postcard" Smith. These are the officers who would lead the troops against Germany in 1914. There is an interesting contrast in the two types of uniform: the Yeoman in old style dress and Royal Horse Artillery in modern uniform. Since the South African war, there had been arguments about uniform styles and whether it should be the more practical khaki or the highly visible red tunics.

(S. Perry collecton).

"OFF TO WAR", 12th September, 1914

Five weeks after the outbreak of World War 1, the support for freshly recruited troops is evident from the enormous gathering in Station Road. In the background, a brass band is visible near the guard's brake van, behind which the driver of the Grand Hotel carriage has stopped to observe proceedings. The smiles on the faces of many in the crowd shows that the full understanding of the horror of war had not yet been realised. This photograph makes one wonder whether the cameraman got down safely from his precarious perch on what was most likely to have been a carriage roof. (See also Volume 2, pages 89 and 90).

(S. Perry collection).

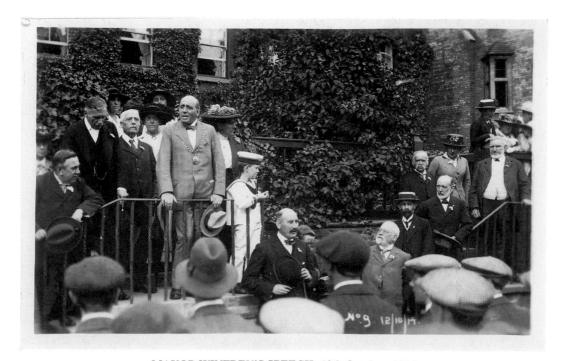

MAYOR WINFREY'S SPEECH, 12th October, 1914

The postcard shows the Mayor's recruiting speech on the steps of the Cathedral Precincts. All those on the "platform" are wearing small single white chrysanthemums. How innocent was the general opinion that the war would be over by Christmas.

(R.J. Sturgess collection).

CHURCH PARADE, 6th December, 1914

F Company, 5th Essex Regiment, were billeted in Peterborough between 1914 and 1915. The first Church Service was held at St. John's Church, Church Street. Here, the procession is making its way down Westgate. On the immediate right is the Westgate Motor Co. garage and then H. Trollope, clothiers, which is on the other corner of the Queen Street junction. After the initial service at St. John's Church, the soldiers marched to the Cathedral for an address by the Dean, whereupon many said that the City had suddenly become a "City of Khaki". This procession was the first of many, as over 3,500 troops were in winter training quarters in the area. As well as the 5th Essex, there were units from the East Anglian Reserve Division, Norfolk and Suffolk Army Service Corps, 4th and 5th Battalions, Norfolk Regiment, 1st and 2nd East Anglian Field Ambulance.

(J. and V. Bull collection).

Funeral of The Late P'te Best, 5th Essex b.

THE FUNERAL OF PRIVATE BEST, 14th January, 1915

Private William Best of the 5th Essex Battalion, was one of the soldiers quartered at Peterborough. He was billeted with Mrs. House at 164, Cromwell Road, and was only in the city a few weeks. He was a qualified band master and an excellent musician. He was very popular, especially with those who frequented the Barrass Memorial Hall social room. On 10th January, while with a party of friends at the Commercial Hotel, Narrow Bridge Street, he was suddenly seized with an attack of paralysis; he never regained consciousness and died the next day. Private Best was buried on 14th January, with military honours. The funeral procession was witnessed by 5,000 citizens, and the service was conducted by Rev. C. Curtis of St. Mark's at Broadway Cemetery, three volleys were fired over his grave and the Last Post was sounded.

(J. and V. Bull collection).

EDITH CAVELL, 1865–1915

Edith Louisa Cavell, was born in Swardeston, Norfolk. She served as a pupil teacher at Laurel Court – Miss Gibson's private school for girls – in Peterborough, from 1884 to 1885. Later, she became a volunteer nurse and, after the German occupation of Belgium, she remained in Brussels to nurse the wounded and helped over 200 Allied soliders to escape. The Germans arrested her and she was condemned to death. On the morning of 12th October, 1915, Nurse Cavell fainted prior to her execution by firing squad. When the German soldiers hesitated to shoot her, an officer took out his revolver and, leaning over his victim, deliberately shot her. Her body was brought home and buried in the grounds of Norwich Cathedral. On 9th December, 1916, an Irish blue marble tablet, in memory of Nurse Cavell, was unveiled in Peterborough Cathedral.

(J. and V. Bull collection).

HOME !
In aid of the Funds of the Local Branch of the National Federation of Discharged and Demobilised Sailors and Soldiers.

A SOLDIER'S RETURN, c. 1919

"Join the Federation today and join other comrades that expect a land fit for heroes on their return home after 1919". Local research has failed to establish who founded the Federation of Discharged and Demobilised Sailors and Soldiers. They were probably a local charity or a similar organisation to the wonderful services provided by the British Legion and the Soldiers, Sailors and Airmen's Families Association. This postcard also prompts the question: why the local drawing of the Guildhall – and was it drawn by a local artist? If so, it is likely that Frank Ball worked for the local newspaper.

(S. Perry collection).

THE FIRE SERVICE, 1905

Members of the Peterborough Fire Service were photographed after winning a hose-cart competition at Raunds. Keen firemen have served the city for years, either as Volunteers or Corporation firemen. One wonders whether these men were under the command of J.C. Gill and rode on the "Clifton" or were Volunteers, just learning to use a new Shand Mason 250 g.p.m. steamer. Men that have worn this uniform have frequently included members of old Peterborian families such as Whitsed, Clarabut and Vergette.

(R.J. Sturgess collection).

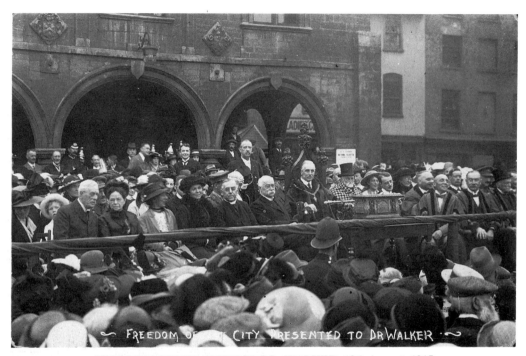

~ FREEDOM OF THE CITY PRESENTED TO DR WALKER ·~

FREEDOM OF THE CITY FOR DR. WALKER, 18th August, 1915

The oak casket was made from Cathedral timber by John Thompson and contained the scroll granting the Freedom of the City to Dr. Walker – the top-hatted gentleman in a check shawl. The ceremony was held on the 18th August, which was the same date as Dr. Walker's eightieth birthday. This was the first time that a Peterborian had received this honour. Dr. Walker was a surgeon at the Infirmary for 43 years, a J.P., and wrote definitively about the French prisoners at Norman Cross. He died in July, 1916.

(R.J. Sturgess collection).

GEORGE G. GREENWOOD, c. 1912

Having won the seat in 1906, Mr. Greenwood retained it in the 1910 election – but with his previous majority of 1,150 votes reduced to just 303. Majorities in the city have always been small. (See also Volume 2, page 85).

(R.J. Sturgess collection).

MR. GEORGE G. GREENWOOD.
The Officers of the Peterboro' Liberal Association
send Best Wishes for the New Year.

J. A. HERBERT,   H. B. HARTLEY,   W. THORBURN,
PRESIDENT.   HON. SEC.   AGENT.

GENERAL ELECTION, 1924

The Market Cross and the cobbled bricks identify this location as the Market Place. A crowd awaits the result of the 1924 election. Did these faces light up at the news of "no change", with Mr. Brassey elected for the fourth and last time? Ramsey MacDonald's government, elected only a year before, collapsed because of the Campbell case. During World War 1, Peterborough had lost its own representation, when it was amalgamated with part of the Northants division, so maybe the local elections failed to generate much interest in the city. In 1929, a Labour government was elected.

(R.J. Sturgess collection).

Area No ....

Date as post mark

Polling District ....

.... Section

Dear Sir (or Madam),

A meeting of the above Committee will be held on

.... *the.........inst., at...... p.m.*

in the .... when

your attendance will be appreciated.

Yours faithfully,

Hon. Sec.

"Our Member"
LORD BURGHLEY

LORD BURGHLEY, MEMBER OF PARLIAMENT FOR PETERBOROUGH, 1931–43

The postcard was used to call the "faithful" to meetings during Lord Burghley's twelve years in office. He went on to become Governor of Bermuda, and became the Marquess of Exeter in 1956. All this took second place to his sporting exploits: in the 1928 Olympics, he won a gold medal for the 400 metre high hurdles; in the 1932 Olympics, he gained fourth place in the same event and won a silver medal for the 400 metre relay; he held eight Amateur Athletic Association titles; he completed a 400 yard circuit of the deck of the Queen Mary in 58 seconds and, in the challenge run made famous by the film "Chariots of Fire", he sprinted round the quadrangle of Trinity College, Cambridge, – whilst the clock struck twelve – in just 44·9 seconds. He was everyone's hero!

(R.J. Sturgess collection).

BAPTIST CHAPEL FIRE, 1905

In October, 1905, the Chapel was completely destroyed by fire. This is a poignant symbol of the fire – the bible is open at II Kings 8, which fails to yield a quotation to soften the blow of this disaster. It does, however, seem to suggest the feelings of the Baptists, who lost their fine Chapel, built 35 years earlier. (See also Volume 1, page 22 and Volume 2, pages 95 and 96).

(R.J. Sturgess collection).

CHURCH ARMY MARCHES, c. 1920

A number of different marches were undertaken to strengthen both the faith and the funds. They were sometimes pictured on postcards – yet, they are not seen very often. This march began in Peterborough, finishing at Cleethorpes and Morecambe. The first destination was easy – the second not so. This postcard has extra interest because of the wonderful array of different uniforms.

(R.J. Sturgess collection).

(4) G.N.R. MOULDERS STRIKE. PETERBORO: 1913.

GREAT NORTHERN RAILWAY, MOULDERS STRIKE, August, 1913

Forty foundrymen of the Great Northern Railway Foundry, situated in Westwood Street, came out on strike after a colleague was dismissed for throwing a blank cartridge into a hot ladle. The strikers refused to return to work until their workmate was reinstated. The strikers also alleged tyranny by a foreman. The picture shows strikers escorting "blacklegs", who remained at work. This ritual was performed daily, as the "blacklegs" made their way to and from the foundry. Although the strikers lost the day – through lack of Union support – it was a foretaste of things to come with the railwaymen's attitudes towards their appalling working conditions.

(S. Perry collection).

WESTGATE RIOTS, August, 1914

Just after war was declared in August, 1914, there was a riot when some of the townsfolk attacked shopkeepers with German names. This comic postcard was bought to reinforce that prejudice. It is postmarked 11th November, 1914, at Helpston, so it was sold after the riots had settled down – but not before profit had been gained by local shop-keepers, from the sales of such postcards. Valentines of Dundee published this postcard, which is marked "Printed in Great Britain", to emphasize that German printers were not involved. Previously, most British postcard firms had had their cards printed in Germany, where there were many specialist printers. (See also Volume 2, pages 86 and 87).

(R.J. Sturgess collection).

ANTI GERMAN RIOTS AT PETERBORO
MAY 14TH 15

WESTGATE RIOTS, May, 1915

This picture shows the aftermath of disturbances on 14th May, when Frank's butchers shop, in Westgate, was attacked. It had previously been damaged in the riots in 1914. Just after 9 p.m., a crowd – mainly soldiers – had gathered and increased to an unmanageable size. A volley of stones shattered the windows of the shop. The atmosphere was intense, but police and military acted with restraint. The Mayor appealed for the crowd to act with traditional English justice. This policy of forebearance succeeded, and soldiers returned to their billets; the streets were quiet by 11 p.m. The damage amounted to about £30 and was charged to the ratepayers. Later that year, for the sake of public peace, six German residents of the city were rounded up and taken to an internment camp in Cheshire.

(J. and V. Bull collection).

92

RAILWAYMEN'S STRIKE PROCESSION, October, 1919

The Railwaymen's general strike started on 26th September, and brought Peterborough to a virtual standstill, as over 3,000 railwaymen, mostly employed at the New England works, walked out. They occupied the wagon works, and Moy's works decided to close down on the 30th September. Other city works, such as Peter Brotherhood's of Walton, and Barford and Perkins of Queen Street Ironworks, only just managed to stay operational; their stocks were greatly depleted as new deliveries were held up by the railway shutdown. The national strike was eventually settled on 5th October. The picture shows a procession of railwaymen and their families marching to the Guildhall to hear the news officially. The marchers are about to turn Lincoln Road Corner, into Westgate. Elm's Garage can be seen in the background.

(J. and V. Bull collection).

NEW ENGLAND CLEANERS ON STRIKE, 1919

Photographed by the fountain at New England, the picture shows the railway cleaners with their slogan "Led but not driven". Many are wearing the Rail Union badge, and two men are holding small flags. Three men are wearing trilbys but the other fifty-one are wearing flat caps. Although the caption does not give a date, this is likely to be the railwaymen's strike of 1919 (see previous page). All the local strikes were broken by "blacklegs".

(R.J. Sturgess collection).

PETERBOROUGH SHOW, 1911

A thousand words would not do justice to this very rare postcard. It was produced by C.E. Mowle of Gorleston for Singer's to use as sales material at the Peterborough Show. A Singer sewing machine was a prized possession in many a household. A special show price of £5.12s.0d is displayed here – this would have been the equivalent of two weeks wages for a clerk and five weeks wages for a labourer. The royal portraits are displayed on the backdrop because it was the same year as the Coronation of King George and Queen Mary.

(R.J. Sturgess collection).

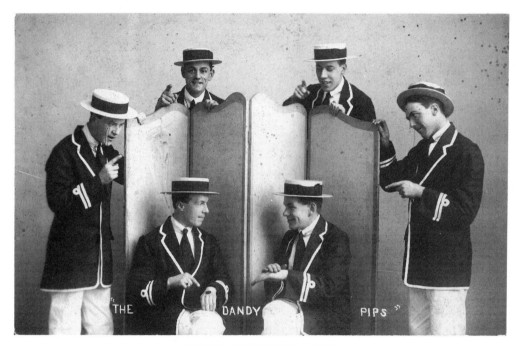

"THE DANDY PIPS", c. 1910

Stanley & Co. of Manston House Buildings, Peterborough, took this photograph of a "fine and dandy" act that appeared around town. Notice the reproving fingers for gambling in public – "heads and tails" for pennies was not allowed, even behind a screen. If caught, a fine of 7/6d was expected, at the discretion of the local magistrates. Here, the monocle denotes the "silly ass" of the party.

(R.J. Sturgess collection).

OPENING OF BRIDGE FAIR PETERBORO OCT 1ST 1912.

BRIDGE FAIR, 1st October, 1912

The Peterborough Advertiser used to print numerous complaints about the "amount of evil and drunkeness during fair week", which always took place in the first week of October. Of 1912 it was said that "Aquarius, in a Puritanic fit, summoned all his forces to put down the fair, which comprised of drinking booths; canvas arcades housing hardware; gingerbread and coconut stalls; wax museums and numerous oyster and shellfish dealers. At the close of the 1921 fair, the police reported that, for the first time ever, there had been no complaints of pickpockets! Since 1874, several members of the Council walked to the fair from council offices but this custom had lapsed during the World Wars. In 1945, the Mayor, Mr. J.A. Farrow, revived the custom and walked from the offices in Bridge Street to the fair, to proclaim it open.

(J. and V. Bull collection).

MEMORAL HOSPITAL CARNIVAL PARADE, c. 1929

This card depicts one of the Hospital Carnival parades which raised funds for the War Memorial Hospital. Joseph Stevenson was then honorary secretary to the Fund. The foundation stone was laid in July, 1925, and the hospital was opened in June, 1928, by Field Marshal, Sir William Robertson. The building was a memorial to the men who had fallen in World War 1; it had 154 beds. It was not fully completed until 1929, when the children's wing was added; this was opened by Prince George. The carnivals included trade stands and this postcard shows the exhibit of Watkins & Stafford, furniture makers.

On the left is a van belonging to A.B. Gibson Ltd., provisions importer and merchants, of Deacon Street.

(J. and V. Bull collection).

PETERBOROUGH OPERATIC SOCIETY, c. 1922

Postcards of amateur productions always turn up with the minimum of information on them and are extremely difficult to research. Yet, every collector knows that there is someone out there who can supply some further information. This is the best card from a series of six, and shows a 1920s production of "Les Cloches de Cornville". Can any reader identify these players?

(R.J. Sturgess collection).

FANCY DRESS BALL, CO-OP HALL, WESTGATE, 6th February, 1918

The Peterborough Equitable Industrial Co-operative Society Ltd. was established in 1877, with registered offices at the Central Stores, Park Road. By 1922, there were 23 branches, in all parts of the City and district, extending over five counties, and 23,000 members; the annual turnover was £780,000. The President and Chairman, at that time, was Thomas Laxton. The Co-op Hall was in Park Road, and the assembly room, situated above Westgate House, was hired out for various functions. It was also the area headquarters of The Trades and Labour Council, and the Unionist Club used to meet in the hall before moving to 77, Broadway, now known as the Conservative Club. On 6th February, 1918, a fancy dress ball was held and the imaginative range of costumes are seen in this photograph. After World War 2, the hall was converted to a restaurant.

(J. and V. Bull collection).

YE OLDE ENGLISHE FAYRE IN AID OF PETERBOROUGH HOSPITAL, 27th – 29th May, 1930

East Ward had a target of £5,120 to contribute towards the total of £100,000 needed for the New Hospital. Being £1,711 short, they held a three-day fair and these worthy ladies supported and ran the twenty or so events. Here is the cream of gentlewomen of the city, all dressed as dairymaids. Every one of their names is listed in "The Fayre Book". It reads like a list of the best local tradesmen with just a sprinkling of the aristocracy as openers. "So buy our things, and see our shows, and bring our labours to a close. Then thanks to us, and thanks to you, The Hospital will have its due".

(R.J. Sturgess collection).

A CRICKET TEAM, 1905

The local cricket team are lined up for a group photograph. Arthur Rose, an all-rounder, is the batsman standing next to the portly umpire. Other family photographs show Arthur as right-back of the Peterborough City Football Club, during the 1908–09 season. This is an indication of the high level of his sporting prowess in both cricket and football.

(R.J. Sturgess collection).

CARTES DE VISITE, c. 1890

Before picture postcards first appeared in 1894, studio photographers sold these cards at 3/6d. a dozen, and had done so for forty years. Postcards, at ½d. each, quickly removed cartes de visite from the market. Somewhat neglected by collectors, the backs are often as collectable as the fronts. There were several studios operating in the city. Larger sizes were available – known as cabinet cards.

(R.J. Sturgess collection).

STUDIO PORTRAIT BY T.S. WILSON, LINCOLN ROAD, c. 1905

This studio portrait is a fine example of the postcard that replaced cartes de visite. The postcard was cheaper, larger and, after July, 1902, could be sent through the post with a message on the back. The fashion content, accessories and personal charm of this small lad provides a fine social history document. It takes dressing-up to new heights!

(R.J. Sturgess collection).

104

BOURGES. — Vue Générale prise du Palais Jacques-Cœur   *Collections ND Phot*

TWIN TOWN – BOURGES, c. 1910

A rooftop view of Bourges, this is typical of pre-1914 French views – sharp and plenty of detail. In spite of its isolation in the fens, Peterborough has lent its name to ten other places in the world and is twinned with towns in Germany and Spain. The city also twinned with Bourges – at their invitation – in 1956. Both places have fine cathedrals and a blend of farming and industry. In Peterborough, Bourges Boulevard now takes most of the traffic that used to pass along Lincoln Road.

(R.J. Sturgess collection).

COMIC POSTCARDS, c. 1906

These postcards are taken from the "Stile" series, published by B.B. of London, and illustrate perfectly the fanciful humour of the Edwardian era. Postcards were far more popular at the turn of the century than they are now; most homes had an album and almost everyone sent cards to friends and relations to show where they were visiting or where they lived. Also, many commercial businesses made use of the cheap postcard rate to send acknowledgements and advertisements.

(J. and V. Bull collection).